The Birthday Effect

JEAN PROKOTT

Published by Black Sunflowers Poetry Press
www.blacksunflowerspoetry.com

ISBN: 978-1-8382516-2-8

TABLE OF CONTENTS

INTRO NOTE

Black Sunflowers called out and from across the globe, poets answered.
The cries of being and feeling were strange, funny, primal, otherworldly,
and angry. Poems raged and fluttered, moaned and muttered, soared and
stumbled. From all the speakings, this voice was heard.

Enjoy,

Geffen Bankir
Amanda Holiday

OUR PROBLEMS ARE THE SAME SIZE AS US, AND THAT'S OKAY

Our houses are never clean, but we're not too worried about it.
Our oil needs to be changed, and we'll do it tomorrow, or maybe Friday after
work.
We're fatter than we want, but Cheetos exist, so there's nothing we can do.
Our bank accounts are embarrassing, and I'm out of fucks to give.
It only snowed two inches, so we can leave it until it melts.
We sleep in too late, but the sun has betrayed us many times.
Our student loans are immortal and blood-sucking, so we'll keep getting
transfusions.
We're hemorrhaging money anyway, casual hundos here and there.
Our animals are extensions of us, and you know what, we're not sorry for
that.
Sure, they run away. But if the gate is open, you take the opportunity.
If the snow bank is high enough, you climb it and jump over.
We drive around and look for each other. Bones will lure us back.

CHANGE IS INEDIBLE

a typo

I am between
the ages of 38 and 8000.
my wings are wood planks
and I spit up time
like Gerber peas.

indigestion of minutes
makes me a bloated
hourglass, disjointed
digital numbers.

who will we be
in 10 years, in 29, in 30.
how gray will I be,
how bald will you,
how fat will we?
how many bedsides
will we weep at,
how often will we visit
graves or hold ashes
or plant trees
        —which one of us
will die first
which one
of us will die first
which one
will miss the other
will it be
too painful to live

which one
will eat
alone—

dear, I must compost
this existential dread

   to feed our vegetables.
I will thaw my memories
and heat them
like leftovers
in a buffet of time—

the recurring dream
when I have too much
dessert and never
enough plate.

we bide time
until meals consumed.
we plant our small garden
and cross our fingers
for growth.

the June strawberries
survived the rabbits,
so we pick their red teeth.
we pinch jalapeño stems
and balance wrinkled Earths
of overripe tomatoes in our palms.
we always over-plant.
some of this food
will go to waste.

together,
we harvest
        and wonder
now what

ON THE 20th ANNIVERSARY OF MY ATTEMPTED SUICIDE

I add a semicolon tattoo to my floral sleeve; it's a dot and wink punctuation puncture of the almost-suicide; it says *your sentence almost ended and here's a beginning*; the semicolon could be an accident: a pair of dark moles, a vampire scar, an uncapped pen; I'd stockpiled pills; it was three days before my 18th birthday; the Prozac capsules were yellow-turquoise-shiny-plastic handfuls of Barbie doll shoes like traffic in my throat; thirteen years later, we gave it a name: bipolar II; it is the mild salsa version; it is independent clauses on each side, depressed and hypomanic; I'm jumping off buildings; I'm jumping over buildings; sometimes I bird-perch on the semicolon to stay warm; I don't remember much about it, to be honest; but imagine being dead for 20 years; or alive for 20 more;

"S" TRAIN

1.

I recognized a ghost in a recent obituary, a man I went on two dates with
ten years ago. It's the thin blond hair that triggered the memory. He'd
kissed too hard. He'd tried to convince me to climb into his backseat in
a bowling alley parking lot and then begged. He was drunk, and I said
goodnight—left him there with his car, knowing he would not call a cab
or a friend.

2.

There are mysteries in our lives we don't know need to be solved, but
then I saw him again with that obit summarizing his 38 years. Since
our last date, he'd stayed with a corporate job, gotten married, had a
couple of sons, and had taken, at some point, a nice picture: smiling,
round cheeks holding glasses, boyish face. Then, he took his life, and
that is all I know.

3.

I promise I am not trying to hijack his story.
I am just wondering when he'd boarded the Suicide Train.

4.

Once I boarded, the *chugga chugga chugga chugga* was the diesel of
my heartbeat. I have been riding for some time, but you don't have to
get off, ever. Sometimes you sit in the caboose and order a sidecar, or
you wander the aisles, or you sit in the dining car and pull on your
hangnails while you wait for that little iceberg salad with four
croutons to come. Most of the time, the trip is so smooth, I don't
realize I'm riding.

5.

Sometimes, I watch the green world pass out the window and wonder
How to be part of it from this side of the glass, clutch my gut and bend
over in hot, numb pain, and heave sobs until my throat is scraped raw
like a fish just filleted.

This comes from nowhere: just suddenly there's a whistle.

Yet, like most of us, I'm still on the train. I keep the possibility of
Getting off locked in my chest, in morbid comfort. *Just in case, just in
case.*

Some of us do that, have travelers' insurance.

6.

But some of us—some of us jump off. When it happens, riders
emerge from our small cabins, open the door, feel the wind pull
and put one foot outside and then the other. We reach for them,
mouths agape, while the wind whips at our hair, but we only see
the blur of their fall.

7.

Goddammit, we are burning this down for you.
We understand, but you've gotta come back.

8.

I dream of him that night, baby-fine hair. We carry matches. I
carry matches…

I'VE BEEN TRYING ON PANTHEISM

for the last couple of weeks, pulling
on the philosophy one leg at a time

like everybody else.

I'm trying to see God in everything
in case that's where he's hiding.

It's always the last place you look.

Point at something. That's God.
Spinoza saw him this way. He said
he was "God-intoxicated." Man, I'd love

to be drunk on holy.

        But obviously,
God is mostly trees. Because
every time I tell my students
to turn a concept into a metaphor,

they turn it into a tree. Grammar is a tree.
Hamlet is a tree. We might as well

call it philoso-tree—branches like neurons
reaching for pain or pleasure to react to,
and leaves, too, green ones that change and fall

to the ground. Students go deciduous
every time.

Pantheists believe in universal substance:
both intelligence and matter, and it creates

out of itself. I can't see it.
I can only imagine more "me"s

coming off of me, tiny blonde heads bubbling
and splitting skulls in mitosis. I can only imagine God

hiding in his tree, peeking out through a small
eye slit in the trunk. He has been assigned

the non-speaking role of "tree" in the school play.
He is sweating under his costume,
waiting backstage for his cue call.

THE BIRTHDAY EFFECT

You (yes, you) are 6.7% more likely to die on your birthday.

when I die on my birthday,
which is the day after the first day
of summer

it will be the second-longest day of the year,
which is good
because you'll have more time
to mourn.

in June, the sun is the same color
as the birthday candle's flame
that jerks from its waxy perch,

and the day melts to dusk,
which gathers in plastic pools
on the landscape of buttercream.

when I die on my birthday,
there's .00018% chance it'll
be because I fell out of bed that morning

or 1.6% chance it'll be suicide,
because God, I hate my birthday
ever since my mother threw me a party

and we played that game where
you sit on balloons until they pop
and you win if you pop the most—

I remember wearing all pink,
standing stubborn in the grass
while girls-I-sort-of-knew

from school popped and giggled
and popped and little latex
empty rainbow gall bladders
scattered the front lawn.

oh, I thought that was so stupid
and my mother tried so hard.
we hit the piñata with a yardstick

       and everyone *had fun*
but I just gathered my candy
like beach shells that all were beautiful
and retreated into myself
and wanted to never
birthday again.

when I die on my birthday,
it probably won't be suicide.
I think I'll get shot by a toddler—

those gremlins kill 52 people a year—
or I'll fall off a boat and hit my head
on the side (626)
and my blood will mix

with the pastel circles of gas fumes
because people are often
on boats in June, at dusk, swatting

mosquitos, which also might be
what kill me (1 million),
or when I die on my birthday,
it will be when I accept the cancer

because hey, I've reached a milestone
so might as well quit while I am ahead
before it erodes my bones (1,550)
or my breasts (40,610)
or my colon (50,260)
or my lungs (157,423)
or my eyes (330).

and when I die on my birthday
celebrate the day after the year's peak,
the highest sun,

the first day of descent.
put all of my birthdays in a museum
or plant them as trees

or fill the gall bladders
and send them to the sky

FATTY, FATTY, 2 x 4

for my middle school bully, who died by suicide

can't fit through
the bathroom door

        actually, we're on the bus
and you can barely fit

        Bully, bully,
        we were haunted
        by the same monster,
        and he wanted us to die.
        Who found you, hanged?
                You tied your magic cape
                around your neck.
        I put my head down
        and smelled my garlic sweat.

fatty, you can't even fit in the seat

look at your rolls
you can't even zip your coat

        I need a pesticide for my shame—
        or just any poison.
        What do I remember about you,
        Noah?—I was on the bus first,
        you found me in the back.
        I watched your sneer, your red gums,
        as you walked down the green aisle.

here comes the bride
all fat and wide

fatty, fatty, pants too tight
look at all that cellulite
I think she has her period
I can smell it

fatty, fatty kill yourself

you could eat
all of McDonald's
lunch ladies fear her
fatty fatty want some candy
drink this Slim Fast first

look at her
she doesn't walk
she waddles
fatty, fatty kill yourself
she's going
to get blood on the seat

      I stopped eating for a while,
      I learned to run, and I did it at night
      so no one would see.
      My God, stereotypes are lazy.
      My God, I'm tired.
      Bully, Noah, did your future dead self
      find you one day, to give you a reason?
      Mine did. I tried a knife,
      made thin, red stretch marks
      on my wrist that scabbed over
      like Morse code embroidering,
      I tried pills, drank charcoal.

      Noah, Noah, two by two
      the animals are boarding you
      your ark, your ship, afraid to drown
      your water, your ghost,
      your monster
      sticks and stones
      your buried bones
      my buried bones
                I'm telling my mom
                but I've got a beautiful face
      oh look you made her mad
                I understand
                and I am so, so sorry.
      your noose, your ship
      what you didn't know
      about the undertow

      what we didn't know
      about the undertow

DEAR READER,

There are many things I want to write poems about
and none of them are grief. But here we are,

dear reader, lying in bed, watching the star projector
circle its fuzzy shapes across the ceiling. It is a toy meant

for a toddler. I bought it after another death,
and still two years later, when I know the bad news,

I wipe its dust, plug it in, and follow the crescent moon,
shaped like a banana, as it disappears and circles back.

Here comes the banana, I say. Sometimes, to be funny, my father
says, *I have a good memory, but it's short.* I wonder if I too suffer

from this affliction. All you can hope for is a highlight reel
as you lay dying. Until then, hold your grief in your hand

like a quivering, hot star. Grief, hand, banana, star.
The projector turns, turns, muffled heartbeat

waves. Banana, fear, star, grief. May I be alone?
Reader, could you be a dear, could you give me a minute?

ANOTHER POEM ABOUT TREES

Yesterday on public radio: an interview
with the guy who updates the leaf foliage maps.

He drives up I-35,
circles a lake—
which is looking less glassy
and more giant cataract—
and bends down

like the goddamned King of Nature

to judge fallen leaves.
Brittle like an old wine cork means
less Big-Bird yellow and more
last week's macaroni & cheese,
and a rubbery bend means maroon.

He pulls out his fall map,
a Paint-by-Number,
and he algorithms how long
until those hidden reds
flare up like endometriosis.

 and I'm like

> *fuck you, Leaf Guy.*
> *that's the best job ever.*

How is there a job in this world
to watch every tree explode
in puberties of paint
and tell listeners like me—*hey,*
moron, go outside
and look at how beautiful this is
at exactly [this time] in exactly [this place]?

> And this morning on public radio:
> it is now legal to compost human remains.

We can lay our bodies
on wood chips, alfalfa, straw—

and in a month become two wheelbarrows
of soil.

A tree can grow from my bones.

Leaf Guy's algorithms
are the human story,

and we can follow his maps
to find each other.

Today, he looks at trees,
and he tells us when they're dying.

Tomorrow, I'll look at graves,
and I'll tell you when they're living.

LOVE LETTER TO IUD

I don't think about you
unless I am thinking
about you.
You fit into the palm
of my doctor's hand:
a bird, wings stretched,
on-the-go dental floss,
hairpin,
small missing piece
from a child's toy.
She shows me
on the 3D model
how you will form
a perfect *T* in my uterus,
a girl finding
her balance on a beam.

META-POSTPARTUM

I came as a six-legged horse,
cobalt cold,
Picassoesque Man o' War

       carrying a jockey made
       of bubblegum and branches,
       my entire life muted fanfare,
       a race lost to Upset.

       in the race
       between woman and man
       my breasts hold me back—
       azure and cinderblock.

I came as indigo as time,
riding a balloon
the balloon was filled with glass—

I came as stiff as seized gears
I greased the pinions with acetone
the acetone was on fire—

I was born sapphire,
and I don't know why
I'm here.

I iron my cornflower cape
and question joy.

Unhappy birthday to me,
I come as an ocean,
navy and bored.
I will major in lazy

and become a galaxy—
hold stars
between my fingers

       I got baby reds
       I got baby greens
       I got baby blues

HOW I MET BEETHOVEN IN THE PSYCH WARD

1801, and Beethoven changes his mind,
writes a note *to* the pianist: *senza sordino*
through this first movement, these pianissimo triplets.

Tells the musician to treat whole notes like casual puffs
on a cigarette, to hold on until he is ready to let them go.
There is no *accelerando*, only more notes,

narcissistic triplets, obsessing over themselves, *one*-two-three,
tripping over phrases, developing, then giving
up, like procrastination.
   In *quasi una fantasia*

Robbie played me *Moonlight Sonata* on the yellowed
keys of the Yamaha upright in the dining hall,

settled the creak of the bench, watched his foot find
the pedal. He pushed his hospital ID to the middle of his forearm
until it stretched, and began to chop a melody, *forte*. Forcing

the notes, common time. The left hand more anxious
than the right. I blinked hard at these awkward rhythms,
these up-and-down-stair climbing notes. Not at all what Beethoven

intended. Not what Rellstab heard as he walked along
Swiss Cantons in the moonlight, not what he saw as a boat
floated like music on Lake Lucerne. When Robbie missed

an accidental, he pounded his palm flat on the keys.
Keep going I told him, and closed my eyes to this unrehearsed
interpretation. Because everything is beautiful

when they don't let you leave. Even among the grunts
of a frustrated stranger, I drowned in Beethoven's
love song, which is often argued a funeral hymn.

I was 17. This was about me,
even as he pinky-plucked the song, the triplets repeating,
the weakest three fingers of his right hand forming the melody—
the weakest part of him creating this music—
which as written looks easy, yet is so hard to play.

ANTHROPOMORPHISM

Our dogs killed a rabbit this morning.
Its scream was like a bird caw,
and I saw them tugging the toy, distinct white tail,
until they disappeared behind the garage to finish the maul.

My husband took care of it.
He held a black, heavy-bottomed garbage bag, and I imagined
the crumpled carnage inside.

    "What was it like, did they eat it?"
    "No, but they ripped its belly open. Its guts were spilling out.
    There's blood on the back fence, if you want to go see."
    We looked to the dogs, bonded pair on the couch.

I keep thinking back to the fight,
the fur in their teeth.
What have I done
to raise such carnivores?

Brian cracks,
"maybe they did it for Mother's Day,"

and now I wonder if this should factor in
to our decision about whether we'll have a child,
because we can't decide.

If this were a Stephen King novel,
I'd get pregnant, but it would be rabbit babies,
and they'd try to claw out of my uterus.
Or I'd be making my morning coffee a week later
and a bloody cotton tail and bones would fall into the pot

Later, I scroll through my phone, and Brian asks what I'm looking at.
    "I want to know if the internet says our dogs are evil."
    He says, "I already Googled that. We're fine.

I don't let the dogs near me
for the rest of the day. I give them side eye,
whisper "murderer, I hate you," when they saunter into the room,
I say "what the fuck is wrong with you" as they squint at me
from their sun-square.

I lift their lips to examine their teeth,
and they comply. And at night, they win again.

We cuddle in bed. I stroke Pepper's black fur.
We have a one to one, human nose to Labrador nose.
"We're not going to do that anymore, okay?"

The Dachshund, Beaker, burrows under the covers,
and I pull them up to survey him in his blanket cave.
"That's not who we are," I tell him.

I WATCH A DOCUMENTARY ABOUT THE PANAMA CANAL WHILE ON AMBIEN

All of life is trying to get on the other side.
God, if it just weren't there:
the hymen of Central America.
We want to tear through,
we want to snap it like a carrot
fresh from the garden
or rip through the tendon
of its jerky.
Its 20,000 dead Frenchmen
appear in my dreams. The fog settles,
a moving cloud of malaria,
and the living room lives.
Minnows swim between my ears,
and I wait for the dirty water
to flood. The white pillow,
a turtle, bows his head in prayer;
the coat sleeve waves,
the room rocks like a small ship,
I argue with the suitcase in the corner.
Dark figures disappear
when I angle my head.
The Panamax of sleep scrapes
my skull. The next morning,
I remember I've made treaties
that Columbia refuses to ratify.
And what *don't* I remember?
The landslides dumped soot
into my trenches.
All those nights hallucinating.
The prescription refilled.
Maybe the suitcase and I
finally made up. Maybe I knelt
before a dark figure and begged
for forgiveness. Maybe I asked
the white turtle to carry me
while I floated along
the two mile canal,
three hours of labor,
until it delivered me
to the other side
and I busted
into that new ocean.

I AM A SALMON, I AM NOT A SALMON

A company called *Whooshh*[1] created a vacuumed tube, and they called it the Salmon Cannon,[2] and without it we would surely have a salmon famine.[3] The fish swim toward the circle-tube-end, which obviously represents a vagina,[4] and reverse-birth themselves home, which is the place they've been looking for the entire time.[5] Before the Salmon Cannon, there were Salmon Stairs,[6] a Salmon Truck,[7] and a Salmon 'Copter,[8] but nothing was so fast as the Salmon Cannon,[9] and nothing was so misty,[10] and nothing was so fun. If we do not cannon, stair, truck, or helicopter the salmon, they swim into turbine blades[11] and are chopped into fishy bits, and if they are not chopped into fishy bits by blades, they stare up, see 551 feet of dam,[12] and think *well, hell, where are we supposed to go now?*,[13] because they've imprinted on the other side, where they were born.[14] So, the lady salmon lay their eggs in warm water, or they lay no eggs at all, and they swim in circles.[15] But at the Roza Dam,[16] salmon find the 150 foot tube in groups[17] and are sucked in together,[18] stretch 100 feet high, and pop out the other side[19] in this new birth.[20] The fish fly, slippery like pineapple spears, and they are home, and maybe someday they will be snatched by bear or pinched in eagle talons and flown high above the earth, just one more time again.[21]

---

[1] It sounds like it sounds.

[2] They must be poets.

[3] I am a poet.

[4] I am a literature student, too.

[5] I am a salmon, too.

[6] And at the salmon gym, a salmon stair-climber.

[7] Not driven by salmon.

[8] Not flown by salmon.

[9] 22 mph.

[10] Like your thumb over the garden hose when you make rainbow, rainbow, rainbow.

[11] If only someone would cannon me away from the blades—but I am not a salmon.

[12] Salmon can see ultraviolet light, which humans cannot; salmon can see beyond the violet.*
   Beyond the Violet is the perfect salmon band name.

[13] How many times have I said this, too?

[14] I drove by my childhood home, and the lawn needed to be watered.

[15] Their slick bodies are moving crescent moons.

[16] In Washington.

[17] I would only travel the Salmon Cannon with you, fin in fin.

[18] The tube can carry 40 fish at a time.

[19] Like a tennis ball out of a ball machine.

[20] When they hit the water, it is a second baptism.

[21] Because with every birth there is every death.

THE SECOND-LARGEST EAR OF CORN IN THE WORLD

We can see it
from our kitchen window,
and I know you're thinking
you lucky bitch!
At night, it's lit
from the bottom
—a rocket ready to leave this world behind—
and some nights
I crawl out the window
and board. I climb
its spindly legs,
pass the green husk,
and hike the yellow skull teeth,
which are painted
with *L*s in the corner
to mimic the kernels'
gleam. Maybe I'll dive
inside, swim in the 50,000 gallons
of water meant for all
of Rochester.
Maize God!
The unanswered
Google question asks:
what is starting wage?
The city wants to tear
it down, and I wish
we'd eat it instead
and see raw gums
rather than empty space.
I bought a shirt with its picture
on the front. It says
Eat Local.
The Second-Largest Ear of Corn in the World
has 4.3 stars on Google.
The one star review:
it's not real corn.
The five star:
I expected nothing, and it gave me everything.

THE OBITUARY

Redwood Falls Gazette: *Kathleen Dehmlow (Schunk) was born on March 19th, 1938 to Joseph and Gertrude Schunk of Wabasso. She married Dennis Dehmlow at St. Anne's in Wabasso in 1957 and had two children Gina and Jay. In 1962 she became pregnant by her husband's brother Lyle Dehmlow and moved to California. She abandoned her children, Gina and Jay who were then raised by her parents in Clements, Mr. and Mrs. Joseph Schunk. She passed away on May 31st, 2018 in Springfield, Minnesota and will now face judgement. She will not be missed by Gina and Jay.*

ginaandjay understand/ we grow from little stems/ that mothers nurture or drown/ Ask yourself/ how will you live your life/ when your mother dies/ (how do you live your life/ because she is dead?)/ The only thing ginaandjay say/ is It's Different/ which is code for I Don't Care/ which means What Will You Do About It/ But Kathleen has something/ to say about the dim light/ present in us and her shadow/ which had gone for a joyride/ which she sewed back on/ to try to be/ herself again/ She was broken too too broken/ no more a hurricane than cirrus clouds would be/ She wasn't flying/ just running/ away/ The sunset was rotting/ into the horizon/ the spiderwebbed storms were warning her/ She was training her happiness/ by whispering/ what it wanted to hear/ And when she saw/ the last days of her life/ when she heard the monologue/ from life's groom/ she needed to know/ if she was a good mother/ If going by the definition/ provided/ then/ no/

THE CITY WHERE PEOPLE GO TO DIE

In the Federal Medical Center, three blocks from my house, the
          government
puts the prisoners about to die: murderers with melanoma, killers
          with colon

cancer, tax evaders with tumors. The Toxic Pharmacist used to stay
there,
that guy who diluted all the chemo drugs: mo' money, mo' cancer.

The guy who sent everyone pipe bombs in the mail was there, too.
My friend says Jim Bakker used to stay there, praying to get out,

or maybe praying to stay in. My friend says, *stop freaking out*

about living so close to the place. Prisoners try *to get there.* The
          facilities are better.
If your heart stops, Mayo Clinic is right up the street—

they'll cuff you to the bed, get you sewn up and back to behind-the-
          bars.
Some people are able to accept the cancer and move on,

pour a glass of beer, sit in their worn-down chair, watch the game.
This is them, but in matching blue uniforms.

Life is a series of difficult choices ending in death. When it
          thunderstorms
here, when the universe cracks its giant shell on the lip of
          Rochester's bowl,

I wonder if the prisoners feel like the storm is trying to break in.
The prison is across from East Park. I run past every day on the
          nature trail,

and the curved barbed wire fence forms crosshatch patterns
on the pavement when the sun hits it right, a giant tic-tac-toe.

My first time through the park, I thought I saw tombstones,
bodies-of-prisoners-past—but they were just sets of horseshoe pits,

as though any of this had to do with *luck*.

BIG, FAT PREGNANCY LIES

The Union soldier, they say, was shot through
his testicle and the bullet lodged into
the fallopian tube of the woman standing behind him.
Virgin birth, he does the right thing, marries her.

The 1920s rabbit test: inject your urine under the white fur.
If she lives, no baby, if she dies, you'll convince yourself
you can feel the baby moving inside of you.
You're afraid to sleep stomach-down.

The Atlantic states in 1934: girl swallows octopus egg
in the ocean. She cramps in her gut, feels the pinch like someone
has tied her intestines in a knot and keeps pulling tighter.
Eight tentacles grow. Somewhere else, some girl pregnant from the
pool,
who knows who the father is. His sperm swam through the
chlorine—
hounds looking for a scent.

1965, the great New York blackout, the *zhoom* of the lights
powering down, the refrigerator stops humming, then
heavy-breathing-groping in the dark, hot breath on a tender neck,
limbs intertwined. *Let's do it again, the lights are still out.*
All those babies nine months later, born of darkness and boredom.

And when it's a mistake, the *shake and shoot* method. Coca-Cola
spermicide, Dr. Pepper douche. Put your thumb on the bottle
and shake, spread your legs, stuff the lip of the bottle inside.
When you're done, you can get 5 cents return.

Or, maybe you should've tried girl-on-top, or sex on the rag,
or maybe you should've taken 20 aspirin afterwards,
or jumped up and down, your bare, flat feet hitting hard,
or maybe you should've sneezed after.

The first lie your mother tells you while you've got a mouthful
of watermelon, a snowball of pink dripping down your chin:
if you swallow a seed, you'll grow a watermelon in your belly.
Your stretch marks zebra like the thick, green rind.

ACKNOWLEDGEMENTS

The author is grateful to the following publications, in which poems in this collection originally appeared, sometimes in slightly different forms:

Angel City Review — "Dear Reader"
Anomaly — "Meta-postpartum"
Arts & Letters — "The Birthday Effect"
Dressing Room Poetry — "Big, Fat Pregnancy Lies"
Minnesota English Journal — "Our Problems Are the Same Size as Us, and That's Okay"
Quarterly West — "How I Met Beethoven in the Psych Ward"
RHINO — "The Obituary"
Sunbeams — "The Second-Largest Ear of Corn in the World"
The Vitni Review — "Love Letter to IUD"
The Laurel Review — "I watch a Documentary about the Panama Canal While on Ambien"
"Another poem about Trees"
"I am a Salmon, I am not a Salmon"

"On the 20th Anniversary of My Attempted Suicide" is anthologized in *A Tether to This World: Mental Health Recovery Stories,* Main Street Rag Publishing Company

"How I Met Beethoven in the Psych Ward" won an AWP Intro Journals Award

"The Second-Largest Ear of Corn in the World" won second place in the Joan Ramseyer Memorial Poetry Contest

"The Obituary" was a finalist for *RHINO*'s Founders' Prize
"The Obituary" comes with gratitude to American Literature Honors students

"I Am a Salmon, I Am Not a Salmon" won the John Calvin Rezmerski Memorial Grand Prize and "I've Been Trying on Pantheism" won the Story Portage Award with the League of Minnesota Poets

Black Sunflowers Poetry Press

Backed by an array of artists, activists, poets and poetry fans from all walks of life, Black Sunflowers, the UK's first crowdfunded poetry press, came into being in March 2020 with a pledge to publish and promote the work of women, older women and black poets from the UK and around the world. Black Sunflowers is grateful to Nat West's #BackHerBusiness scheme, all the supporters including Patrick Bill, Amanda Sebestyen, Cathy Greenhalgh, Rehana Zaman, Rob Curry, Nadine Marsh-Edwards, Rosa Fong, Judah Attille, Elinor Perry-Smith, Monika Baker, David Curtis, Oona Hyland, Janice Cheddie, Simone Alexander, Mustapha Feika, Michael Cadette and others who wish to remain anonymous, as well as the additional enterprise finance awarded to us. Black Sunflowers is thankful to those who have offered encouragement and advice along the way and who have contributed their skills or inspired through their own publishing entrepreneurship.

Embarking on this venture during Covid19, on the cusp of a lockdown was challenging and perhaps folly. Yet, with daily life on hold, this has been a time for deep reflection for all of us. A time perhaps to pause for poetry.